Emily Arnold McCul

Our Little Mushroom

A Story of Franz Schubert and His Friends

Margaret K. McElderry Books

New York London Toronto Sydney New Delhi

Our friend Franz auditioned for the emperor's choir school when he was eleven. He barely spoke a word, but he sang like an angel. When we burst into applause, Franz's face turned red as a rose.

We students called him "Schwammerl," our "Little Mushroom." He was very small and quite round. His talent amazed us, but he was so shy! And so absentminded, often forgetting his cap, his homework, or his lunch.

In Vienna everyone loved music. The Schubert family had a string quartet. Franz played violin and viola. He longed for a piano, but the Schuberts couldn't afford one.

We found a piano warehouse and that's where Franz practiced. He was already composing.

By the time he was sixteen, Franz had written several hundred compositions—operas, symphonies, quartets, masses, chamber works, but most of all, songs. They simply poured out of him. He couldn't afford music paper, so Josef bought it for him.

Franz told his father he wanted to become a professional musician.

"It's too hard. You'll starve!" Herr Schubert shouted.

He ran a school in their home,
and he made Franz teach the first
grade. Our friend tried to write songs while swarms of six-year-olds climbed
all over him. It was mayhem. There was never a more passionate composer. We
couldn't bear to see his gift wasted.

"Don't visit Franz again!" Herr Schubert ordered us. "You're a terrible
influence!"

We made a vow: we would all help him devote himself to music. He was the
most talented of us all!

We sent Franz a message: "Come with us. Together we will live for art! We won't let you starve." Some of us grew up to be poets. Others were painters and one a playwright. Most of us earned small salaries in government offices, but we lived for our art. We kept telling Franz he could live for his music. And so, after many months, Franz left his father's school.

He needed a place to sleep. Moritz's mother offered her spare room. But Franz's habit of composing into the wee hours disturbed her.

He moved to Johann's. And then to a rooming house kept by the other Franz's mother, Frau Sanssouci. He wore his clothes and eyeglasses to sleep, so he could jump right out of bed and compose in the morning.

Before long, Franz began setting our poems to music. Our words suddenly gained astonishing power when they became songs! Some were joyful and some mysteriously sad. All of his melodies were achingly beautiful. But only we heard them.

Gradually, we realized his father was right. A composer had to be supported by a rich patron. A concert could attract a patron, but concerts cost a lot of money. . . .

We bragged about Franz's beautiful melodies to everyone. Count
Esterházy was impressed and invited him to his country estate to give
piano lessons to the talented Esterházy sisters.

Franz told us that he was living like a god, even though forty geese were honking outside his room and he couldn't hear himself speak! The piano duets he composed for the girls were sublime.

When Franz came back to Vienna, he moved in with Eduard. Their room was so small, they had to take turns working. Franz would hold entire compositions in his head and then, when it was his turn at the desk, write them down as fast as he could.

We friends kept asking ourselves, what more could we do to make Franz's splendid music known to the rest of Vienna?

Then we had a stupendous idea: we would hold little concerts of Franz's music in peoples' houses. They wouldn't cost anything.

We made up a name:

Schubertiade.

Twenty people came to the first one. Franz played the piano, and Josef sang. After the concert, there was feasting and dancing. We played charades, and read each other's poems. It was a glorious evening!

Forty people came to the next Schubertiade. To the following one, more than one hundred! In good weather we had picnics and games outside after the music.

Soon, the tide was turning for our Little Mushroom. Our circle
of friends was swelling. Franz was becoming famous. A hotel played
Schubert songs on its mechanical clock. Publishers printed his music.
He was asked to compose for churches, birthday parties, and plays.

In 1827, Franz's lifelong idol, Ludwig van Beethoven, died. Franz was picked to carry one of the torches in the long funeral procession.

"Who will stand beside Beethoven?" one of the mourners asked sadly.

"Franz will," we assured him. We were certain his music, too, was immortal.

But Franz had been hiding a secret from us. He was ill. Sometimes he couldn't get out of bed. Astonishingly, the flow of glorious music increased.

We friends realized we mustn't wait any longer. We pooled our money and hired a theater so that Franz could finally have a public concert!

Franz selected the program and asked the finest
musicians to perform with him. They all accepted.

When the box office opened, tickets flew! By the day of the concert, March 26, 1828, the theater was sold out. His father and all his family were there. Afterward, the audience leaped to its feet, nearly delirious with joy.

Franz was so shy, we had to drag him out to take a bow . . .
followed by many more bows.

There were stories in newspapers as far away as Berlin. "Beethoven was a genius; Schubert is a miracle," wrote one critic.

Franz knew he might never be well again. He said to us, "Nothing can make me forget the happy sweet hours I spent with you."

He often seemed his old merry self, so when he failed to attend a party, we worried. In the fall of 1828, Franz's doctor ordered him to go to his brother's house and stay in bed. He never got up again.

Weakly, he asked to hear Beethoven's String Quartet No. 14 in C-sharp Minor. Then he fell into a delirium. We heard him whisper, ". . . Beethoven is not here."

On November 19, 1828, our Little Mushroom died. He was only thirty-one.

His brother told us he had composed fourteen songs in his last weeks. They were dedicated to his friends.

Despite our sorrow, we were proud that his ravishing, heartbreaking music no longer belonged just to us. Now it belonged to the world.

AUTHOR'S NOTE

During Schubert's lifetime, 1797 to 1828, Vienna entered a period of domestic happiness and security called the Biedermeier. For all the jolliness of the era's coffeehouses and dance halls, there was disappointment, too, in the lack of democratic reforms.

The Viennese emperor's minister, Klemens von Metternich, maintained peace and staved off more unrest by censoring, or preventing one from viewing, all the arts. Schubert and most of his friends met secretly to share their work. Once, their meeting was raided by the secret police and Schubert spent the night in jail. One of his friends was exiled.

Because it was difficult to discern subversive messages in a piece of music, that was the art that flourished most in Vienna. Beethoven, Gluck, Czerny, Salieri (accused of poisoning Mozart), Haydn, and Schubert were all popular. Private homes of well-off families nearly all contained pianos. Music was performed everywhere by amateurs and professionals alike.

Schubert had auditioned for the court choir because its school offered the very best academic education. But his father discouraged a music career for his prodigy. In fact, a career in music was (and is) very difficult. But Schubert couldn't help himself. He had to compose— and he never compromised in order to please the public. He labored all his life in the shadow of Beethoven. "Who can do anything after Beethoven?" he asked one of his friends.

Lyric poetry, a poem typically written in first person that discusses personal feelings, was the favorite genre of Schubert's contemporaries. When it was set to music, it was elevated to the lied, or song. Schubert's songs carried romantic themes—loneliness, wandering, yearning, death—to new heights with inventive and beautiful harmonies, so much so, he is considered the inventor of lied.

Most of Schubert's pieces for orchestra were never performed during his lifetime, so Franz never actually heard them; nor, of course, did anyone else.

A few of his friends later admitted that the Schubertiades had in some ways exploited, or taken advantage of, Schubert. He never earned a penny at a Schubertiade and played until his fingers ached while everyone else listened and danced. But Schubert loved to play and, as far as we know, didn't complain. His circle later recalled his "boundless modesty," his being "all aglow for art" and a stranger to "falsity and envy."

Had Schubert lived, would his one major concert have supercharged his career? Perhaps not. As it happened, the virtuoso violinist Niccolò Paganini gave a series of concerts right after Schubert's. They were all Vienna could talk about for weeks on end.

After his death, Franz's friends presented one more concert of his works, a memorial, and raised enough money for a tombstone. They gathered up his great compositions and put them away for safekeeping in cupboards and closets. Every year, they saw to it that more works were published, surprising and delighting the music-loving world. Franz had written one thousand pieces of music, including eleven operas, two melodramas, half a dozen symphonies, several masses, dozens of quartets and piano pieces, dances, cantatas, and some six hundred songs. Pieces were discovered over the next 150 years.

All along, it was his friends who sustained him and made sure his music wasn't lost.

BIBLIOGRAPHY

https://www.chambermusicsociety.org/about/news/schubert-and-his-social-circle/

https://www.google.com/books/edition/The_Cambridge_Companion_to_Schubert/pWMgAwAAQBAJ?hl=en&gbpv=1&dq=Schubert+Memoirs+by+His+Friends&pg=PR13&printsec=frontcover

Deutsch, Otto. *The Schubert Reader: A Life of Franz Schubert in Letters and Documents.* New York: Norton, 1947.

Gibbs, Christopher. *The Life of Schubert.* Cambridge: Cambridge University Press, 2000.

Listen to major pieces composed by Schubert:
https://www.udiscovermusic.com/classical-features/best-schubert-works-10-essential-pieces/